The world premiere of THE DEATH OF IVAN ILYCH was produced by Denison University Theater in Granville, Ohio, on 16 April 2004. The cast and creative contributors were:

IVAN ILYCH .... Jon Farris
GERASIM .... Vasilios Yani Koumandarakis
PRASKOVYA .... Megan Long
LISA, VOICES, GHOST BRIDE .. Elizabeth Martinez-Nelson
VASYA .... Rankin Langley
VOICES, DOCTOR #1, TUTOR, GHOST GROOM
.... Drew Lichtenberg
VOICES, DOCTOR, DOCTOR #2 .... Michael Akira Sato
VOICES, DMITRI, PRIEST .... Chris Carr

Director .... Dan Bonnell
Set design .... Brad Steinmetz
Costume design .... Cynthia Turnbull
Costume design assistant .... Sarah Casebolt
Lighting design .... John Edward Ore
Sound design .... Andrew Johns & Dan Bonnell
Video artists/technicians
.... Christian Faur & Trent Edwards
Technical director .... Andrew Johns
Director's assistant .... Daniel Carr
Stage manager .... Brooke A Aldrich
Assistant to the author .... Sarah Broderick

MISE-EN-SCENE

What follows are details of the attempt to translate and transpose the literary elements of a world-masterpiece, Leo Tolstoy's *The Death of Ivan Ilych*, into a modern dramatic equivalent of the tremendous 1886 original.

The profound difference between a "Literary" and a "Dramatic" narrative is made painfully clear each time we are confronted with an adaptation to film or stage that is all the more frustrating and disappointing for our elevated expectations and long loyalty to the beloved original work itself.

There are, of course, "literal" adaptations or "Readers' Theater" word-for-word renditions, and these may be highly enjoyable "Masterpiece Theater" type productions. But as they are neither *masterpieces* nor *theater* in their own right, they are bound to fall short of their cathartic imperative of instigating terror and pity in the breast of the viewer as the original author has done in that of the solitary reader.

What we are generally treated to are elaborate, even spectacular "Cliff Notes" of the work of art itself. Thus, *Anna Karenina* must play itself out as nineteenth century moral melodrama. In the case of the Vivien Leigh, Ralph Richardson film, we enjoy a rich and splendid melodrama, but a melodrama nonetheless. In short, we have delivered to us the grand, familiar, obligatory, cautionary plot—but with only microscopic

THE DEATH OF IVAN ILYCH
© Copyright 2004 Donald Freed

All rights reserved. This work is fully protected under the copyright laws of the United States of America. No part of this publication may be photocopied, reproduced, stored in a retrieval system, or transmitted, in any form or by any means, electronic, mechanical, recording, or otherwise, without the prior permission of the publisher. Additional copies of this play are available from the publisher.

Written permission is required for live performance of any sort. This includes readings, cuttings, scenes, and excerpts. For amateur and stock performances, please contact Broadway Play Publishing Inc. For all other rights please contact Patricia Rae, pattyraef1@aol.com, 310 472-6530.

Cover art by Stephen Farris

First edition: April 2004
This edition: September 2017
I S B N: 978-0-88145-236-5

Book design: Marie Donovan
Page make-up: Adobe InDesign
Typeface: Palatino

THE DEATH OF IVAN ILYCH

*Donald Freed
from the writings of
Leo Tolstoy*

BROADWAY PLAY PUBLISHING INC
New York
www.broadwayplaypublishing.com
info@broadwayplaypublishing.com

clues to Tolstoy's genius narrative of finitude and existence, itself. *Lolita* on stage must be pornography; *Babbitt*, farce; Trollope's *The Way We Live Now*, soap opera—inferior to a mediocre pastiche like *The Forsythe Saga* when it is serialized for television; *Crime and Punishment*, a Christ-ridden police procedural; *The Divine Comedy*, a *grand guignol*.

If the translation from Literary to Dramatic is ever to be achieved, the secret must be in transposing the author's narrative from the Literary to the Dramatic voice. That is, to bring the Literary voice down to a lower order of abstraction, the Dramatic, and then to unleash the non-verbal visceral libido of this action that churns beneath the surface of the original author's symbolic linguistic strategy on the novel's page. This lower order of abstraction contains the third dimension of the living actors/characters on the stage. On the page, Count Tolstoy writes that Ivan Ilych screams for three days in his death agony. On the stage we hear that scream and our hair may stand on end: a lower order of abstraction.

The dramatist who redacts Tolstoy's life and death of Ivan Ilych must pursue what T S Eliot called the "Objective Correlative" to the sub-text or inner monologue or narrative meditation of the original work of art; pursue the libido or soul of the masterpiece and translate into action, gesture, stage time and space the existential or dramatic equivalent of the printed page.

If in the novel the Plot must always progress in one direction—forward—while the Narrative is driven in an opposite direction or angle—backward through the protagonist's life and memory, against the grain of the Plot—then it is the unbearable tension of this existential dialectic that excites and finally explodes the catharsis and the purgation in the psyche of the reader. But can this eruption take place with the same power in the theater , in the collective unconscious of the audience? The answer should be yes if, and only if, the translator/playwright can find, in action, the Dramatic Objective Correlative for the narrative and subjectivity of the original Literary music which, alone, is the signature of genius.

Tolstoy's unequalled lifelong exploration of the depths of life and death lies hidden in plain sight under our nose. The plot—a man's illness and death—is as commonplace as the "The King Must Die," or "Boy Meets Girl"—plots, *all* plots, are a dime a dozen and as old as the hills. The challenge is to find the Third or Dramatic dimension that is the soul of the Literary masterwork and transport it back onto the stage—where it was born long before modern storytelling found the literary or novel form.

Time and Place: A District Capital in Russia, 1882

As the Civil Councilor, Ivan Ilych, sickens and dies, his mind and memory return compulsively to his childhood, youth and early maturity. These over-determined (deeply conflicted) memories and images are the icons of the dying man's life.

The young Ivan Ilych should be played by the actor who will also play Ivan Ilych's thirteen-year-old son, Vasya.

Each memory scene is dated, and played out in only light and space. The same memory or scene may become increasingly distorted or tortured as Ivan Ilych sinks into the "Black Bag" of death.

As the plot's timeline moves inexorably like a fever chart forward towards the end, the narrative memory-line twists and turns like memory, itself, back and forth. The logic of the plot is as elemental as $1 - 1 = 0$: "Death". But the narrative nostalgia is wildly eccentric, non-rational, illogical, associative and dreamlike:

Mise-En-Scene

"Life". The plot is sheer biology; the narrative, the depths of psychobiology: the soul.

There is no intermission or interval.

Setting: On a proscenium stage there should be a four-foot high platform, Center, with steps leading up on either side.

Centered on the platform is a leather couch, with small tables at either end.

Above, behind, and surrounding the platform are media screens. On these screens will be reflected the year of the scene in progress, as well as landscape or visuals in reference to the memory of scenes from the past. Also displayed on the screens are dreams, nightmares, terrors, longings: the subjective correlatives to Ivan Ilych's physical decline and decease. On these "Epic" screens, the internal organs of Ivan Ilych appear in anatomy-chart color and contour.

The space around the couch, on the platform, can be broken into a lighting plan that includes interior candle and oil lamp light; and sun and moon beams through shuttered or framed windows, depending on the season and time of day or night.

Scenes from the past, memories, dreams, should all be played off the platform in specially-lighted areas, so that the empty stage is nothing but space and time in the "Black Bag" of Tolstoy's vision of life, death, the soul, and finitude.

Sound: Each scene has its own soundscape, ranging from the mundane to the surreal, depending on the state of Ivan Ilych's body and soul in any given sequence.

CHARACTERS

IVAN ILYCH GOLOVIN, *middle-aged, member of the Court of Justice, judge*

PRASKOVYA FEDOROVNA GOLOVINA, *forty, wife of* IVAN ILYCH

LISA GOLOVINA, *twenty, daughter of* IVAN ILYCH *and* PRASKOVYA FEDOROVNA

VLADIMIR IVANICH (VASYA), *thirteen, son of* IVAN ILYCH *and* PRASKOVYA FEDOROVNA

DIMITRY FEDOROVICH, *forty-five, brother of* PRASKOVYA FEDOROVNA

GERASIM, *twenty-five, a peasant house servant*

DOCTORS, *middle-aged, high professional pomp*

Colleagues, visitors, servants and dramatis personae as required. In some cases, "voices off" may suffice.

Doubling: All characters may double, except for IVAN ILYCH. *For example: young* VASYA *for the* YOUNG IVAN; PRASKOVYA FEDOROVNA *for the* YOUNG IVAN ILYCH's *mamma; the* DOCTORS *for* IVAN ILYCH's *brother-in-law,* LISA's *fiancé, and various memory and dream figures, etc.*

(*Before the house lights dim, for some minutes, there is the far-off echo of funeral chants from the Eastern Orthodox Church. This ritual fades out as darkness envelopes the audience.*)

(*In the dark, complete silence... Then, like a knife, a scream—and again and again: the short, stabbing cries of a man in the agony of his death throes. The screaming goes on for a full minute, at least. Then, silence, again*)

(*Silence. Then, sounds of male voices [educated, mature; attorneys and judges]. In darkness, general conversation of cards, food, theater, diet, sport, interrupted by someone entering:*)

VOICE ONE: Gentlemen! Ivan Ilych has died!

(*General vocal reaction, then:*)

VOICE TWO: Get away!

VOICE THREE: You don't say so!

VOICE ONE: Here, read it yourself—in the black border.

(*Sound of newspaper rustling*)

VOICE TWO: Mm... "Praskovya Fedorovna Golovina, with profound sorrow, informs relatives and friends of the demise of her beloved husband Ivan Ilych Golovin, Member of the Court of Justice, which occurred on February the fourth of this year 1883. The funeral will take place on Friday at one o'clock in the afternoon..."

(*The voices and sounds fade away, but not before we hear the voices—planning for this evening's "card game at the

Mayor's..."; "I'm on a strict diet..."; "...no, no pastry..."; "...is a gorgeous creature..."; etc.)

Scene One
September, 1882

(*Humming a waltz,* IVAN ILYCH GOLOVIN *strides, like a star actor, into his new salon. The light is bright autumn sunshine. The civil jurist carries a small step-ladder.*)

(IVAN ILYCH *poses himself in the entry way, cocks his head to listen to the sounds of hammers and house cleaning, off. Then he surveys his drawing room and possessions with triumph.*)

(*His court costume is splendid: top hat, light overcoat, cane, gloves. And, underneath: the most elegant cloth, gold watch, ribbons and medals, red sash. Over all, beams the ruddy, neatly bearded healthy face of the Honorable* IVAN ILYCH, *at the height of his powers.*)

(*He begins to whistle another tune as he takes off his hat and coat. Then, he lifts the ladder, with ease, and glides up onto the platform and begins to adjust a curtain rod [pantomime].*)

(IVAN ILYCH *leaps down from the platform like a gymnast; he is the master of his house and his universe. He surveys his handiwork; tours the stage [miming adjustments]. He hums another waltz, executes a few dance steps; strips off his formal suit coat and does an exercise before returning to the ladder, by leaping back up on the platform.*)

(IVAN ILYCH *[in pantomime] attempts to hang a curtain. He climbs to the top step of the ladder, stretches, reaches too far—slips and catches himself, but bruises his side on a [invisible] window handle. He groans. Just at that moment,* GERASIM *is entering and sees his master slip.*)

GERASIM: Ivan Ilych—Excellency!

IVAN ILYCH: Ahh! No, no—I'm alright.

(GERASIM—*making the sign of the cross*—*leaps up onto the platform to help* IVAN ILYCH.)

GERASIM: Master—you should call me!

IVAN ILYCH: Ah, thank you, ah—

GERASIM: Gerasim.

IVAN ILYCH: Gerasim. It's a good thing I'm a bit of an athlete—or I was when I was your age, ha-ha—another man might have been killed or, ah, but I merely knocked myself. Mm—just here.

(GERASIM *makes the sign of the cross and helps* IVAN ILYCH *to sit on the couch.*)

GERASIM: You don't want the doctor, sir?

IVAN ILYCH: No!—ah, that's better. No, my health is perfect. I'm glad my family's not here. They believe in doctors, ha-ha! Ah... You're a strong lad. Ger...

GERASIM: Gerasim... You should call me, Your Honor.

IVAN ILYCH: Gerasim. No, it's nothing. I'm no valetudinarian. What a long word, eh? Ha-ha—I'll teach you, I, ahh—

GERASIM: You should call—

IVAN ILYCH: I know, I know, but my family, they all arrive tomorrow and when I pledge and promise that their "new official residence" will be *tres comme il faut*—you may bank on it! ...So—back to work—in the court hanging criminals, in my new house hanging curtains, ha-ha—except that the family is the harsher judge. Hold the ladder, now—families, ah, Gerasim, you know, families.

GERASIM: Yes, Your Honor.

IVAN ILYCH: You're a strong lad—you have a wife and little ones? (*He descends and puts on his formal coat.*)

GERASIM: No, master.

IVAN ILYCH: Ha-ha, you will, Gerasim, you will!

(Lights out)

Scene Two
November, 1882

(IVAN ILYCH and his wife, PRASKOVYA FEDOROVNA, talk with their family physician. Husband and wife sit on the couch, the DOCTOR on a chair. At the foot of the platform, in shadow, stands the servant, GERASIM. He waits and listens.)

(The gloomy cold early winter light paints IVAN ILYCH's face pale and white.)

PRASKOVYA FEDOROVNA: *(To IVAN ILYCH)* ...I must interrupt, I simply must! It's for your sake, not mine. I'm not the one who can't sleep. *(To the DOCTOR)* His appetite is definitely off—you know what a wonderful eater he was—now, if Lisa is a minute late at table, he falls into a tantrum! He shouts at his son, who's still a boy, he—

IVAN ILYCH: The Doctor does not want to—

PRASKOVYA FEDOROVNA: *(To the DOCTOR)* Nikita Andreevitch, I appeal—

DOCTOR: Ladies and Gentlemen, I beg you—calmly, calmly... Now, then, Judge—this pain in your side: you will recall that I predicted that—

IVAN ILYCH: —That it would grow worse—

DOCTOR: Precisely—

IVAN ILYCH: Before it grew better, and—

DOCTOR: Exactly! And that—

PRASKOVYA FEDOROVNA: —therefore, a—

IVAN ILYCH: "*Specialist*" must—

DOCTOR & PRASKOVYA FEDOROVNA: —be consulted!

(They all burst into hysterical laughter as the Medical Montage begins.)

Scene Three
Medical Montage. December, 1882

(GERASIM carries IVAN ILYCH's heavy winter coat and fur hat as he makes the rounds of the medical elite of the city.)

(On the screen: paintings of IVAN ILYCH's internal organs. Church bells ring.)

(As IVAN ILYCH goes from DOCTOR's office to DOCTOR's office, his wife, PRASKOVYA FEDOROVNA, daughter, LISA, and son, VASYA, decorate a Yule bush next to IVAN ILYCH's couch, on the Platform. Their mood is gentle and happy, their faces bathed in warm firelight. But, in the street, cold green moonlight etches IVAN ILYCH's face.)

(IVAN ILYCH's family works carefully, slowly adding bits of colored paper to the greenery. As they work, they sing softly an old song of childhood [a French nursery melody.])

(Meanwhile, on the screen: IVAN ILYCH's kidney. In a DOCTOR's office:)

IVAN ILYCH: —But what I'm asking is whether or not my case is serious?

DOCTOR ONE: And that is why you must put yourself in our hands so that—

IVAN ILYCH: But first I must know whether or not—

DOCTOR ONE: But my dear Ivan Ilych, the case is exactly the same as in your law court!

IVAN ILYCH: What?

DOCTOR ONE: *Exactament.* In the court—I am in your hands. *You* lay down the law, *you* rule on the order of evidence and its relevance. *Vraimant*?

IVAN ILYCH: Gerasim, we're leaving, call for the sledge!

(*On the platform, the little family, arms entwined, admire their handiwork, as they hum their old nursery song.*)

(*At the same time,* GERASIM *is helping* IVAN ILYCH *into his coat as they leave the first* DOCTOR's *office for the second* DOCTOR's *office.* IVAN ILYCH *curses,* GERASIM *makes the sign of the Cross.*)

IVAN ILYCH: ...Idiots! Scoundrels! Frenchmen! Building houses with my money! The "same as the law court" —How dare he make that comparison?!

(*They have arrived at the second* DOCTOR's *space. On his screen:* IVAN ILYCH's *appendix. Scene begins in progress:*)

DOCTOR TWO: ...But your question—"is my case serious"—is a *non sequitur*. The correct question is: do we have here a case of floating kidney, chronic catarrh or appendicitis? (*Pause*) And my considered opinion is...

IVAN ILYCH: Yes?

DOCTOR TWO: Appendicitis.

IVAN ILYCH: (*Laughing*) Thank God! Simple Russian at last! Gerasim, bow down before a true man of science.

DOCTOR TWO: Now, now, now. Ha-ha. Go home and enjoy your New Year's festivity. Come back and see me in the new year and—

IVAN ILYCH: You will operate and remove these—

DOCTOR TWO: "Objection noted," Your Excellency, as you judges say in the court, ha-ha—first the evidence and then the verdict. In your—

IVAN ILYCH: The appendix is what—

DOCTOR TWO: The appendix is what we *suspect*. But the proof, the *proof* will be in the urine!

IVAN ILYCH: Urine?

DOCTOR TWO: In the u*rine*. After the New Year. We will examine the u*rine*, the evidence, and then, mm, then, mm-hmm...

(On all screens: ice and snow. Family spot out)

(IVAN ILYCH and GERASIM struggle against the howling wind that pulls them about in the street. IVAN ILYCH hangs onto GERASIM to catch his breath. He cradles his aching side. The sun is sinking, the wind whistles.)

IVAN ILYCH: ...Ah, hah...Say nothing at home. Not a word...doctors! Who do they imagine that they are? What? Germans, vampires! ...Let me lean, that's it, you're strong, you're strong... Ahh, not a word, remember, not a word...

(The voices: IVAN ILYCH's wife and daughter are talking, under, as the next scene begins.)

Scene Four
An Hour Later: 4:45 P M

(IVAN ILYCH's wife and daughter—PRASKOVYA FEDOROVNA *and* LISA—*circle the depressed* IVAN ILYCH *as he sits in the middle of his couch, under the decorated holly branch.* GERASIM *stands below the platform in shadow.)*

PRASKOVYA FEDOROVNA: ...It's his own fault! Mind now to take your medicine regularly. Give me the prescription and I'll send Gerasim to the chemist's.

(IVAN ILYCH listlessly hands a paper to his wife, she gives it to LISA who, in turn, drops it down to GERASIM, who runs out.)

PRASKOVYA FEDOROVNA: Lisa, we must go. *(To* IVAN ILYCH*)* I beg you not to sneak that homeopathist in here again while I'm out—oh yes, we know all about it—or that "friend of a friend" —that will make you a laughing stock—with his wonderworking icons, ha-ha!

LISA: Papa, if we have to go to Italy—

PRASKOVYA FEDOROVNA: Lisa, don't—

LISA: Whatshisname, the German specialist, told—

PRASKOVYA FEDOROVNA: Lisa!

LISA: Mamma, it's not our fault! Papa, it's not my fault! *(Pause)* I intend to marry Fedor Petrovich in May, either here or in—

IVAN ILYCH: *Get out!*

(PRASKOVYA FEDOROVNA *and* LISA *flee from* IVAN ILYCH's *roar. Alone, he rises slowly to his feet. He begins to pace like an old man, stares with hatred at the Yule decorations, then lies back down on the couch.)*

(He closes his eyes. In the distance, someone plays Chopin on the piano.)

(GERASIM *tip-toes into the shadows with a bottle of medicine, but exits again so as not to disturb the sleeping* IVAN ILYCH.)

Scene Five
A Dream. 1844

(Church bells, and the piano continues under the dream. On the screens: church and school buildings from IVAN ILYCH's *youth.)*

(While IVAN ILYCH *dozes fitfully on the couch, muttering to himself, in his dream he is, again, in his first year in high school.)*

(Special light up on the twelve-year-old YOUNG IVAN ILYCH *in a tutorial with a grim* TUTOR.*)*

(The boy, YOUNG IVAN ILYCH, *kneels; the* TUTOR *presses down on him. On the couch,* IVAN ILYCH *jerks and mutters throughout.)*

TUTOR: And what is Kiesewetter's logic, you silly little Ivan? *Demonstrato*: "Caius is a man, men are mortal, therefore Caius is mortal." Now—what's Kiesewetter's Logic? Speak up, boy!

(On the couch, IVAN ILYCH *produces a muttered word salad of both voices.)*

YOUNG IVAN ILYCH: "Caius is a man, men are mortal…"

IVAN ILYCH: *(On couch)* "…Caius is mortal…"

Scene Six
Continuous. 1882. 5 P M

(Cross-fade to IVAN ILYCH *on the couch, tossing and crying out.* GERASIM *climbs up onto the platform. His strong movements are quick, quiet, gentle.)*

(The piano is still being played, far off. A yellow [couch special] light produces a jaundiced mask on IVAN ILYCH'S *face.)*

IVAN ILYCH: "…Caius is a man!…"

GERASIM: Master, shh, they'll hear you, Ivan Ilych, master—

IVAN ILYCH: What?

GERASIM: Your medicine, Excellency—

IVAN ILYCH: What's that?

GERASIM: Your wife—

IVAN ILYCH: Shh—not a word!

*(*GERASIM *makes the sign of the cross.* IVAN ILYCH *sits up and mops his face.* GERASIM *spoons out medicine.* IVAN ILYCH *swallows and stands, then begins to exercise.)*

IVAN ILYCH: Mmmh—better. *(Stands)* Better. I'll soon be better. *(Walks)* Doctor's orders. *(Exercises)* Bitter—better, bitter—better, *ein, zwei, drei, ja ja*! Gerasim, tell them I shall go back to the court, after all—

GERASIM: Your Honor—

IVAN ILYCH: *Toute de suite*! I'm feeling ever so much better. My wife knows best, after all, I've only to follow the Doctor's orders to the letter of the law and I'll be stronger than ever. Where's my new coat, ha-ha!

GERASIM: You were having a bad dream, master, but now—

IVAN ILYCH: Nonsense, Gerasim, a happy dream, on the contrary, a perfect dream: It, ah—wait. Mm. Yes. My mother. Mm. Playing the piano. Her white hands. Mamma...

(GERASIM *makes the sign of the Cross. Piano, off, ceases. Silence.* IVAN ILYCH *smiles.*)

GERASIM: Dreams, you know, sir, tell us what will, ah—

IVAN ILYCH: The rustle of her silk dress... The aroma of vanilla...

(IVAN ILYCH *smiles like a child, lost in memory, as* PRASKOVYA FEDOROVNA *and her brother,* DIMITRY, *enter.*)

PRASKOVYA FEDOROVNA: My dear, look who's paying a house call—

IVAN ILYCH: What's that? I don't—

PRASKOVYA FEDOROVNA: No, it's not another doctor, but he's a wise man, ha-ha.

IVAN ILYCH: Ahh—Dimitry Fedorovich— *(To* GERASIM*)* —my brother-in-law, not a word—come in, my dear fellow, I'm completely restored. I've had the most wonderful sleep and dreamt of—days gone by.

DIMITRY: My dear Ivan...Ilych...

(DIMITRY *is dumbfounded as he stares at* IVAN ILYCH's *altered, wasted appearance.*)

IVAN ILYCH: ...I have changed, eh?

DIMITRY: Well, ah...

PRASKOVYA FEDOROVNA: ...He's promised to take his medicine. I'm the one who needs a change. He fell, that's all. A ridiculous accident. That's all. *(Pause)* Gerasim, bring the master his drops. *(To* DIMITRY*)* Come, Lisa's waiting for us, she wants your blessing for her wedding invitation.

(They exit. IVAN ILYCH sags, stares at GERASIM, turns away. The servant exits.)

(Voices can be heard from another room. IVAN ILYCH tries to make out the conversation. As he moves to the corner of his platform to eavesdrop, the words become clear.)

DIMITRY: *(Off)* …must face reality…

PRASKOVYA FEDOROVNA: *(Off)* What are you saying?

DIMITRY: *(Off)* Two months and that's—

PRASKOVYA FEDOROVNA: *(Off)* You're exaggerating.

DIMITRY: *(Off)* Exaggerating! Don't you see it? What? He's a dead man! Full stop. Look at his eyes—there's no light in them. *(He looks.)*

PRASKOVYA FEDOROVNA: *(Off)* That's why I begged you to come! That why I wrote to—

DIMITRY: *(Off)* I know—but what is it that is wrong with him?!

(PRASKOVYA FEDOROVNA breaks into deep sobs and the voices move out of earshot. Silence)

(Slowly, IVAN ILYCH begins to examine himself in the glass [mime glass]—first full face, then profile. Next, he bares his arms to the elbow and studies their morbid reduction. Then, he picks up a photograph from the couch endtable and stares at it.)

(On the screens: the wedding photo of IVAN ILYCH and PRASKOVYA FEDOROVNA. The sound of the piano is heard again from another room.)

(IVAN ILYCH stares at the photograph with tears in his eyes. He is so absorbed that he does not hear PRASKOVYA FEDOROVNA enter. She is stricken at the sight of his anguish. Moves to him, helps him to the couch, puts the photograph aside.)

(Husband and wife look at each other through their tears. She murmurs her intimate name for him.)

PRASKOVYA FEDOROVNA: ...Ivan...Vanya...

(He shakes silently, still looking into her eyes. Then, with trembling fingers, she unbuttons her blouse. He watches like a child. She touches his head.)

(The piano stops. Silence. He leans toward her. Suddenly, a stern commanding voice from the past, over the action:)

VOICEOVER: "Caius is a man—men are mortal—therefore Caius is mortal."

(Husband and wife freeze. Lights out.)

Scene Seven
January, 1883

(In the dark, the autocratic voice continues but, now, it is one of IVAN ILYCH's DOCTORS *speaking to him.)*

(On the screens: images of an appendix.)

(In silhouette: IVAN ILYCH *bowing lower and lower under the* DOCTOR's *injunction.)*

DOCTOR'S VOICE: Vermiform appendix. Verm-i-form. Or floating kidney. *Flo-ting kid-ney. Ja—Ja—Ver-mi-form, haben Sie geschreiben?* We must stimulate the energy of one organ and check the activity of another—the absorption will take place and everything will come right. *Punctum. Comprenez vous?* The flo-ting kidney—we must catch it—

*(*IVAN ILYCH *begins to run from screen to screen, grasping at pictures of kidneys as they appear and disappear from view on the screens.)*

DOCTOR'S VOICE: *Haben Sie geschreiben?* Catch it! Arrest it! *Haben Sie geschreiben!* Support it! Catch it! Arrest it! *Punctum!* Arrest it—arrest it—arrest it!

(IVAN ILYCH *collapses on the couch. The* DOCTOR's *voice is now the* TUTOR's.)

(*On the screen:* IVAN ILYCH's *childhood school*)

TUTOR: Caius is a man—men are mortal—therefore Caius is mortal.

IVAN ILYCH: *(Screams)* But—I am not Caius!

Scene Eight
Continuous. 6 P M

(GERASIM *comes running. Church bells in distance.*)

GERASIM: Excellency, Your Honor!

IVAN ILYCH: I am not...mm. What?

GERASIM: You were calling out in your sleep. God protect us. *(He makes the sign of the cross.)*

IVAN ILYCH: What? Tell me what I said.

GERASIM: You were calling out for someone. Ganya, maybe—you're all tired out from the last doctor, and here's your drops, it's time to—

IVAN ILYCH: Who? Ganya?

GERASIM: Sasha? I don't know. Gius…

IVAN ILYCH: Gius…Caius! Caius…

GERASIM: "Caius." Who's that?

IVAN ILYCH: What time is it?

GERASIM: Just six. Do you want the candle?

IVAN ILYCH: *(Pause)* Gerasim, ah, may I have that blanket.

(GERASIM *arranges blanket, pillows, medicine; bathes his master's face: this strong young peasant is almost maternal in his care and concern.*)

GERASIM: Yes, master, there we are. Now, this, that's right, sit up a little; God be praised here's soup, take a little for God's sake. That's it, God bless you, sir.

IVAN ILYCH: Thank you. *(Pause)* Gerasim—you're a true Christian. Do you have other work to do now? Hm? Do you, ah, have the time to, ah… Do you want to know who "Caius" was?

GERASIM: I have time. Your Honor is ill.

IVAN ILYCH: But I mean, you're running from morning to night, taking me to doctors, and, ah, looking after my, ah, "needs"…

GERASIM: Ah, what's a little trouble when it's only your illness? No trouble, no trouble at all.

IVAN ILYCH: *(Pause)* Thank you, son…Caius…

GERASIM: Sir?

IVAN ILYCH: "Caius is a man…"

GERASIM: Ah. Oh. Well—we're all sinners, Excellency.

IVAN ILYCH: *(Laughs)* A-ha, bless you, boy, bless you. So we are. So we are…. You see when I—can you read, lad, have you been taught?

GERASIM: No, Your Honor.

IVAN ILYCH: Well, Caius…we were taught that "Caius is a man, men are mortal, and therefore Caius is mortal." You understand?

GERASIM: The soup is helping Your Honor.

IVAN ILYCH: I feel stronger, walk with me, let's walk— shall I teach you to read, to reason, to think? Walk, yes, let's walk. *(Pause at window)* Snow…

(IVAN ILYCH *leans on* GERASIM *and they walk around the platform.*)

GERASIM: Thank God, Your Honor is—

IVAN ILYCH: Yes! "Take up your bed and walk." Shall I teach you to read the Gospels?

GERASIM: Wait. Rest, master, not too fast.

IVAN ILYCH: You could study with my son. My Vasya. Poor boy, I know what he's going through at his age... We're all sinners, Gerasim.

GERASIM: That's the God's truth, master. Sit, now, sir.

IVAN ILYCH: Ahh—it does me good. But, ah, my legs, my legs ache.

GERASIM: Put them up, sir—right up on my shoulders.

IVAN ILYCH: What?

GERASIM: Yes, sir, my old grandpa always did.

IVAN ILYCH: He did? Was he, ah...

GERASIM: He did. Like this. That's right. That's better. He did. God rest his soul. He was born a serf.

(IVAN ILYCH's *legs are now lifted up onto* GERASIM's *shoulders. Church bells in the distance. Twilight*)

IVAN ILYCH: Yes...this helps. You're sure you're able to, ah...

GERASIM: Sure, what else should I be doin'?

IVAN ILYCH: Yes. You're quick. You're as bright as my son.... You see, Gerasim, Caius was a mortal man

GERASIM: Yes, sir.

IVAN ILYCH: And all mortal men die.

(GERASIM *makes the sign of the cross.*)

IVAN ILYCH: But now, here is the point: Of course, Caius is a mortal man and must die—that's logic, Kiesewetter's logic, ha-ha! Man, in the abstract, must die—

GERASIM: *(Makes the sign of the cross)* Amen.

IVAN ILYCH: Must die, that's the Second Law of Thermodynamics, Newton's law of—

GERASIM: Huh?

IVAN ILYCH: *(Laughs)* Never mind: "Caius," whoever he was, must die, but *I* am not Caius! *(Pause)* Do you understand?

GERASIM: Your Honor is the Honorable Ivan Ilych of the Municipal—

IVAN ILYCH: *(Laughs)* I love you, son, what a good soul you are! Now, listen to me, it's doing me a world of good to talk. So—now, uh, you comprehend, I know: I am not Caius. I am, as you say, Ivan, ah...but that's not the point. The point is that I was—I was a boy, myself, once, "Vanya" —with a dear mamma and papa—a sister, a brother—my own toys, my own dear nurse, Kalenka - not, ah, "Caius," you see, not at all. No, I had a striped leather ball that smelled of horsehide, and "Caius" did not have that ball—and he did not kiss my mamma's hand, or hear the rustle of her silk dress when she passed...

(GERASIM *wipes away* IVAN ILYCH's *tears.*)

GERASIM: More soup, Excellency.

IVAN ILYCH: We boys, you see, we knew that "Caius" was mortal and had to die. So we were taught. But we, ourselves, we were not condemned, because our case was different from that of Caius—we were not Caius! Do you grasp my meaning, son?

GERASIM: ...Let me rub your legs with the oil, now, sir.

IVAN ILYCH: Do you understand...

GERASIM: I know, Excellency, I know. Certain, we're all sinners, and must all die. *(He rubs* IVAN ILYCH's *legs.)*

IVAN ILYCH: I was Vanya. I was not "Caius." Yet here I am. It's impossible, but here it is! And what's the answer—how can I be Caius—he never existed, he never lived, but I did—look at me, I did, I lived, I had a mamma who tucked me in at night and we said our prayers...So tell me, you nursed your grandfather, and he wasn't Caius either—what did he say, your grandpa, what did he know—did he know the answer?

GERASIM: He was an "Old Believer." I think he knew "something".

IVAN ILYCH: He did!

GERASIM: He used to tell me—at the end—"God sees the truth...."

IVAN ILYCH: Yes! He said that? Go on, what else?

GERASIM: "God sees the truth—but he waits."

IVAN ILYCH: *(Pause)* He waits.

GERASIM: Amen.

IVAN ILYCH: He waits...for what? What do you mean—what did the Old Believers know?

GERASIM: God waits.

IVAN ILYCH: But why! What does it mean. I'll have you whipped!

GERASIM: The Old Believers, all they would say was—"God—you know—God."

(IVAN ILYCH *stares at* GERASIM. *Slowly his eyes close and he loses consciousness.*)

Scene Nine
Continuous. 7 P M

(PRASKOVYA FEDOROVNA *and their son,* VASYA, *and daughter,* LISA, *appear at the Platform.* PRASKOVYA FEDOROVNA *stands on the stage floor,* VASYA *and* LISA *push and shove each other up the steps.*)

PRASKOVYA FEDOROVNA: Shh—shh!

(The children grimace and mime nausea at the odor coming from their father's sickroom. The mother slaps the children, hard, and gestures them out and away. They exit. Silence. Church bells)

(PRASKOVYA FEDOROVNA *very gently steps up onto her husband's platform. He is groaning and whimpering in his sleep. She mimes adjusting the curtains, causing a light change to deep shadows.*)

(She starts to leave but stops to look at her wedding photograph. On the screens: the wedding portrait of IVAN ILYCH *and* PRASKOVYA FEDOROVNA.)

(Wedding waltz, under, as the next scene begins.)

Scene Ten
Spring, 1862

(The dance music is more distant, now. The bride and groom are in a moonlit garden. He stands behind, holding the bride as they both stare up at the moon, seeing their future. His voice is young, warm, resonant.)

IVAN ILYCH: ...They're looking for us.

PRASKOVYA FEDOROVNA: No. One more dance, please.

(IVAN ILYCH *and* PRASKOVYA FEDOROVNA *waltz, then return to the moon.*)

PRASKOVYA FEDOROVNA: You're the best of all the dancers!

IVAN ILYCH: Well, let them find us, then—a man only gets married once, eh?

PRASKOVYA FEDOROVNA: Do you love me? More than anyone?

IVAN ILYCH: More than all the world besides.

PRASKOVYA FEDOROVNA: Is that from a French novel?

(IVAN ILYCH *and* PRASKOVYA FEDOROVNA *both laugh. He holds her tight.*)

IVAN ILYCH: Shall we dance together until the dawn?

(PRASKOVYA FEDOROVNA's *breathing is affected.*)

PRASKOVYA FEDOROVNA: Oh, Vanya, my own Vanya. *(Whisper)* You have to tell me what, ah, I must do.

(IVAN ILYCH *covers* PRASKOVYA FEDOROVNA's *breasts with his hands. She sways. He holds her erect.*)

IVAN ILYCH: Shh, I'll teach you everything. All the steps.

PRASKOVYA FEDOROVNA: *(Pause)* Your past, ah, life...

IVAN ILYCH: You shall hear it—

PRASKOVYA FEDOROVNA: *(Covers her ears)* No! I don't want to, I don't—

IVAN ILYCH: Shh. "*Il faut que jeunesse se passe.*" It was all done with clean hands, in clean linen, ha-ha—

PRASKOVYA FEDOROVNA: No, I do not—

IVAN ILYCH: *Justqu comme il faut*—you needn't worry, little bird, you will never—

(PRASKOVYA FEDOROVNA *breaks the embrace. The music pauses.*)

PRASKOVYA FEDOROVNA: Tell me again about our home.

(IVAN ILYCH *takes* PRASKOVYA FEDOROVNA *in his arms again, as they look out and up at the moon.*)

IVAN ILYCH: Once more and then we're off... Your *bon enfant* is going to be a "New Man." I am a man of the "'60s" you see, and this is the "Age of Reform": new laws, new institutions of Justice, of literature, of Liberalism!

(A new waltz begins.)

IVAN ILYCH: New men are needed, men like me, and I shall be an Examining Magistrate, in a new province, and there—

PRASKOVYA FEDOROVNA: Our home, the house.

IVAN ILYCH: Yes, of course, my darling, and we New Men, we moderate Liberals of the new Legal Code, we Nineteenth Century Men—

PRASKOVYA FEDOROVNA: But when—

IVAN ILYCH: We will allow our beards to grow! Ha-ha! Wait, I'm coming to our house.

(They laugh.)

IVAN ILYCH: The home of the Public Prosecutor—

PRASKOVYA FEDOROVNA: Our—

IVAN ILYCH: House! Yes: I, myself, will choose the wallpapers, the antiques, the reception room, the drawing room, the fireplaces—

PRASKOVYA FEDOROVNA: *(In bliss)* Ah yes, don't stop!

IVAN ILYCH: The dishes and plates, the little screens, the bronzes, the paintings—

PRASKOVYA FEDOROVNA: *(Embracing him)* I love you, Vanya, I love you so!

IVAN ILYCH: "More than all the world besides?"

PRASKOVYA FEDOROVNA: "More than all the world besides!"

(*And* IVAN ILYCH *and* PRASKOVYA FEDOROVNA *waltz away into the night. Church bells up as the action returns to the moment in 1883.*)

(*On screen: the wedding photograph.*)

Scene Eleven
1883, 8 P M

(PRASKOVYA FEDOROVNA *replaces the photograph. Screens go dark.* IVAN ILYCH *starts to wake.*)

IVAN ILYCH: What? ...Who is it? ...Oh...where's Gerasim?

PRASKOVYA FEDOROVNA: He's taken a note to the doctor.

IVAN ILYCH: No!

PRASKOVYA FEDOROVNA: No, not tonight...tomorrow.

IVAN ILYCH: If I had the strength—I would kill them all!

PRASKOVYA FEDOROVNA: *(Pause)* And me?

IVAN ILYCH: And myself, too!

(PRASKOVYA FEDOROVNA *starts to creep down the steps.*)

IVAN ILYCH: Wait. It's so dark. What's the time?

PRASKOVYA FEDOROVNA: Late.

IVAN ILYCH: The morphine—I'm in a fugue—I was dreaming of our wedding.

PRASKOVYA FEDOROVNA: You were? So was I—remembering the waltzes—running through my mind all day.

(PRASKOVYA FEDOROVNA *hums the waltz,* IVAN ILYCH *joins her.*)

IVAN ILYCH: …Over and over.

PRASKOVYA FEDOROVNA: Yes.

(Pause)

IVAN ILYCH: Go.

(PRASKOVYA FEDOROVNA *starts slowly.*)

IVAN ILYCH: No. Wait. *(He hums again.)* What happened? *(Pause)* At first, we were, ah—your caresses, you were so—

PRASKOVYA FEDOROVNA: It's late.

IVAN ILYCH: Please wait… The new crockery, new linen, we were—

PRASKOVYA FEDOROVNA: Don't excite your—

IVAN ILYCH: You were carrying Lisa and—

PRASKOVYA FEDOROVNA: I must—

IVAN ILYCH: —And you were depressed, no, wait, and jealous, you made scenes, you found fault with everything, nothing was—you began to hate me, you—

PRASKOVYA FEDOROVNA: Stop it, Ivan. You'll make yourself ill.

(IVAN ILYCH *laughs.*)

PRASKOVYA FEDOROVNA: You ran away to your club, your card games, your—

IVAN ILYCH: *(Trying to stand)* Light the candle! Light it. I want to see your face. I want to know why you—will you light the candle, for God's sake!

(PRASKOVYA FEDOROVNA'*s hand trembles as she lights the candle.* IVAN ILYCH *coughs, compulsively, and spits into a rag.*)

IVAN ILYCH: Wait...wait... When you couldn't nurse the baby you blamed me for—

PRASKOVYA FEDOROVNA: *(Choking)* You were the Public Prosecutor, the whole world trembled when you entered the chambers—

IVAN ILYCH: *(Coughing)* Go away!

PRASKOVYA FEDOROVNA: No! I'll tell you what it is: you were the Judge, full of power, "All Rise!" And all you needed at home were your "conveniences": dinner at home, entertaining the Governor, Generals, famous actresses—

IVAN ILYCH: Go!

PRASKOVYA FEDOROVNA: Frenchmen and Germans—you only wanted a hostess—

(IVAN ILYCH *coughs.*)

PRASKOVYA FEDOROVNA: —a housewife, a *femme de chambre*—your bed!

(IVAN ILYCH *falls onto the couch.*)

PRASKOVYA FEDOROVNA: Indictments, a fur gown, imprisonment, and your filthy bed! *(She leans on the end table, gasping.)*

IVAN ILYCH: And you hated me!

PRASKOVYA FEDOROVNA: Yes! And you despised me!

IVAN ILYCH: Of course! We despised each other: *Like all married people!*

(Silence. Church bells)

IVAN ILYCH: We became vulgar. *My* court, *your* house, *our* bed: in short, "marriage". War over the children, war—

PRASKOVYA FEDOROVNA: But you were the High Judge!

IVAN ILYCH: *(Laughs, coughs)* Now, it's over—and you've driven me to the wall... The court, the silk robes—all theater. The doctors, the lawyers, the priests—the bride, the groom—theater...

(PRASKOVYA FEDOROVNA *picks up the wedding photograph and hugs it to her bosom.*)

PRASKOVYA FEDOROVNA: I loved you very much... but nothing came of it...Vanya—what do you want from me? What can I do? *(Silence)* If I—have wronged you— I beg your forgiveness—I was just a woman, underneath all the *comme il faut*, just a woman. *(She bows down to kiss her husband's feet.)* Do you want to beat me? *(Pause)* Beat me, if it will help. Beat me!

(He reaches to stroke her hair.)

IVAN ILYCH: Little mother... Listen. I have to tell someone about, ahh, about—"IT". *(Pause)* Put out the candle. Please.

(PRASKOVYA FEDOROVNA *does.*)

IVAN ILYCH: Turn away. Don't look at me. *(Pause)* Praskovya Fedorovna, I swear to you on our children that I have tried to follow the doctors' orders, all of the doctors' conflicting, ignorant orders, and to *will* myself back to health. Read medical books, secretly consulted a priest, *and* a midwife, yes, as God is my judge, *(Coughs)* I went back to the court just as I always had: chatted with my colleagues, talked nonsense, literature, Liberal politics, just the same as always. *(Coughs)* But, then, in the middle of a testimony or a legal opinion, the pain in my side would begin its "gnawing" again— yes, gnawing—and there, in spite of all my will power, there it was: "IT".

(IVAN ILYCH *pants.* PRASKOVYA FEDOROVNA *is framed in the window's light.*)

PRASKOVYA FEDOROVNA: *(A breath)* "It"?

(IVAN ILYCH *forces himself to sit up.*)

IVAN ILYCH: "*IT.*" ...*IT* would come and stand before me—would look at me. "IT." The court chambers would melt away, and only "*IT*" was there. Filling up the court, filling up the world. Do you understand? That when I came home and found a scratch on the table polish and shouted at the servants and then you and Lisa would run in and argue about who was to blame and I screamed at you—that was my only relief, to attack you and for just a moment forget about *IT*—I couldn't control *IT* so I took out all my terror and rage on you and this house! And I would demand, "Let me move the table," and you—knowing nothing about *IT*—would always repeat, "Let the servants do it, you will hurt yourself again"—and, like a flash, *IT* would pop up from behind a screen staring at me! And my side would start its gnawing—like an animal inside me! —*IT* would be peering out at me from behind the flowers or the windowsill. Aghh! Now—do you understand? Do you?

PRASKOVYA FEDOROVNA: (*Overlapping*) No. Beat me!

IVAN ILYCH: You must! This is the truth, the whole truth, and nothing but the truth. Not the "truth" of the court but the truth of *life*!

(PRASKOVYA FEDOROVNA *begins to limp across the platform.*)

IVAN ILYCH: I lost my life over that curtain that I was trying to hang—for *you*—as surely as a soldier who storms a fort.

(PRASKOVYA FEDOROVNA *is at the step.*)

IVAN ILYCH: Terrible, stupid! You don't believe me. You think it can't be true. It can't—but it is. *IT* is!

(PRASKOVYA FEDOROVNA *goes down one step at a time. Her voice is a harsh whisper.*)

PRASKOVYA FEDOROVNA: No—no—no…

(PRASKOVYA FEDOROVNA *is gone.* IVAN ILYCH *sits staring at* IT, *and shaking like a leaf. Church bells, over, and darkness.*)

Scene Twelve
Three hours later. 11 P M

(IVAN ILYCH *considers immediate suicide.*)

(*He sits bolt upright in green moonlight, unconsciously stroking a leather button on the couch. The touch of the leather button brings back the powerful memory of his childhood and his father's leather briefcase. The dying man's breathing fluctuates; he is becoming a boy again. Church bells*)

(*Suddenly, the aroma of vanilla is around him: His Mother!*)

(IVAN ILYCH, *now the boy, is radiant, joyous, ready to die to be reunited with his Mama.*)

(*He begins to hum a waltz, lifts a medicine flask as if it were a magic potion. He is ready to leave this brutal sick room. He pants, gasps in the aroma of vanilla—makes the sign of the cross—sobs with joy…*)

(*Church bells begin tolling. The ghost of* IVAN ILYCH's *mother is gone, and* IVAN ILYCH *is condemned to live through another night.*)

Scene Thirteen
Three hours later. 2 A M

(*Darkness except for a weak, cold moon beam.* IVAN ILYCH *shifts slowly, unable to sleep.*)

(*Out of the silence begins an orchestration of various bells marking the hour: First a soft chime from within the house, then a nearby church bell, then other church bells farther away: All bells signal two A M, but all of the sounds are overlapping or elliptical, none of the bells match each other in timing or tone.)*

(As the contraction of bells spreads, he grows agitated, finally crying out:)

IVAN ILYCH: ...Why are all the clocks wrong!? What time *is* it?!

(Out of the dark silence, a voice:)

GERASIM: Master?

IVAN ILYCH: ...You're here. I knew it! ...Why? Why are you here, son?

GERASIM: *(Pause)* In case.

(The sound of IVAN ILYCH *controlling his breathing)*

IVAN ILYCH: ...Mm, mm. *(A deep breath)* But you're not here—every night?

GERASIM: ...I'm here.

IVAN ILYCH: Mm...two months ago I didn't even remember your name. And, now, here you are. In the cold.

GERASIM: On a blanket. No trouble, Your Honor.

(Silence)

IVAN ILYCH: Spring's coming.... Life'll go on. The, ah, wedding... And you—what will you do?

GERASIM: Stay here.

*(*IVAN ILYCH *pauses, then chuckles softly,* GERASIM *joins in. But* IVAN ILYCH's *soft laugh turns into a cough, then into a paroxysm.)*

(Distant, light piano music, under, begins the next scene.)

Scene Fourteen
Ten Days later. 2 P M

(Cold winter morning light. Cello, off, IVAN ILYCH's *son practicing)*

*(*IVAN ILYCH *is trying to rise from the commode. He stands—too weak to pull up his trousers—in his undergarments, panting.)*

*(*GERASIM *hurries in to help his master to adjust his clothing and to sit down, then the young peasant carries out the commode. Silence, cello;* GERASIM *returns with the cleaned pot.)*

IVAN ILYCH: Forgive me. I'm helpless. It's disgusting. *(Laughs bitterly) Comme il ne faut pas*! And the inside of my mouth is like a trench, the whole room reeks so that the dogs won't even come in anymore.

*(*GERASIM, *to prevent a breakdown, lifts* IVAN ILYCH *to his feet and helps him into his robe; straightens the blanket and linen on the couch; aids the master to lie down; prepares medicine.)*

IVAN ILYCH: Ahh—ugh—the stench—how can you stand it? "The tombs, the tombs, I live in the tombs!" You know your Gospel, son? And what did Jesus say to the madman?

GERASIM: "Come out of the man!" Take this, now, master.

IVAN ILYCH: No more morphine—it's driving me mad… What else? And, ah, "Lazarus", ah—what? I tell you my mind is, ah—what? What did Jesus, ah…. *(He tries to stand.)*

GERASIM: "…and He cried in a loud voice, Lazarus, come forth!"

IVAN ILYCH: *(Laughing in hysteria)* "…Lord, by this time he stinketh: for he has been dead four days…"

(IVAN ILYCH *collapses in* GERASIM's *arms, sobbing with laughter and tears. The peasant youth rocks the dying official.*)

IVAN ILYCH: Stinketh! Stinketh!

GERASIM: "And he that was dead came forth, bound hand and foot with grave clothes; and his face was bound with a napkin. Jesus saith unto them, Loose him, and let him go."

(IVAN ILYCH *is exhausted.* GERASIM *returns him to his couch.* IVAN ILYCH *lies panting and groaning,* GERASIM *gives him water.* IVAN ILYCH *starts to hiccup. His color is sheer yellow.*)

IVAN ILYCH: —Black Bag *(hiccup)* Black Bag—

(GERASIM *hums a child's song.*)

IVAN ILYCH: *(Hiccupping)* —dream every—night—I'm—pushed into a—big—Black Bag—a black *(Hiccup)* sack—

GERASIM: Sure, it's the medicine, you're not yourself, master. Drink a little—that's it. You're not yourself.

IVAN ILYCH: No. I never was. *(Hiccup)* I never was. *(A deep breath)* It's all false, from beginning to end…. When I was a child—but after that, all lies…but "God sees the truth," eh, boy?

GERASIM: Yes, sir—but "He waits."

(GERASIM *and* IVAN ILYCH *both laugh softly.*)

IVAN ILYCH: You're wonderful. You could make me believe again. If only you could read the Gospel to me like, ah, my, ahh—So, tell me about your grandpa. "God—you know—God"—eh?

(GERASIM *and* IVAN ILYCH *laugh.*)

GERASIM: May he rest in peace.

IVAN ILYCH: Amen. "God—you know—God"! ...
School, the Law, Marriage: all lies...

(GERASIM *massages* IVAN ILYCH's *legs. Bells toll the half hour.*)

IVAN ILYCH: *(Softly)* See if anyone's listening. Go on.

(GERASIM *checks. Nothing*)

IVAN ILYCH: No? *(Laughs)* No one...except for you, I'm completely alone. Remarkable: alone in the midst of a populous city—dying of a long Latin word—surrounded by family, friends, colleagues, doctors—and I could not be more completely alone anywhere—not at the bottom of the sea, or under the earth....

(*Off the platform, in a separately lighted area,* PRASKOVYA FEDOROVNA *and* LISA *appear.* LISA *tries on her wedding gown as her mother helps her model it. No dialogue, only the choreography of the nuptial rite and the cello, off.*)

(*At the same time,* IVAN ILYCH *confesses to* GERASIM.)

IVAN ILYCH: You remember—Gerasim—You remember the day it happened, don't you? When I, ah, when I slipped. "Pride goeth before a fall," boy, remember that—ugh! Listen to how I'm preaching and patronizing—I know nothing, absolutely nothing! I've misunderstood it all! Stop, listen! (*He swings his feet to the floor, and grasps* GERASIM's *hand.*)

(*In their area,* PRASKOVYA FEDOROVNA *and* LISA *model the wedding dress.*)

IVAN ILYCH: The truth is—I slipped, I bruised myself, the bruise turned into something else—the doctors, the medicine, the entire charade: You've seen it all, and, ah, you've pitied me. And that's why I'm telling you everything. Do you hear someone? *(Pause)* No. We're alone.... (*Into* GERASIM's *ear*) So, you know, the pain grew worse and worse and, at the same time, my life grew worse and worse. And they're all waiting for me to die. Why not? They want to live—to live! Full stop!

(IVAN ILYCH *snarls with regret and shame. He tries to stand.* PRASKOVYA FEDOROVNA *and* LISA *action fades out, cello out.*)

IVAN ILYCH: The Cadet, the Student, the Law clerk, the Lawyer, the Assistant Prosecutor, the Chief Prosecutor, the Lower Judge, the High Judge. "All Rise!" *(He falls back.)* The Lover, the Husband, the—

(GERASIM *rocks* IVAN ILYCH.)

IVAN ILYCH: "All Rise" —rise… All my "triumphs" turned to lead, to stone. The only bright spot was back there at the beginning. After that, after, ah…it all became dark and black—faster and faster—days and nights on this couch, nights and days scurrying past like black and white mice—speeding by in inverse ratio to the square of the distance from death… *(His head sinks onto* GERASIM's *chest.)*

(GERASIM *lays* IVAN ILYCH *back on the couch, lifts his legs and resumes the massage.*)

IVAN ILYCH: Mmm—that's better—but it can't go on, you have to rest.

GERASIM: Take your time, your Honor.

IVAN ILYCH: …It's the lies that're poisoning me, not you, you make everything, even this room, sweet and clear, ahhh…

GERASIM: Go on, I'm listening.

IVAN ILYCH: …the great lie: that if only I would listen to the doctor—that what's happening to me is merely "routine"—you know—visitors, tea in the morning, newspapers, sturgeon for dinner, the weather—and I want to scream at them, "Stop your stupid farce—you know that I know that you know—that I am dying!

GERASIM: *(Rubbing hard)* Talk on, talk on, Ivan Ilych.

IVAN ILYCH: They talk and chatter—"Sarah Berhardt will be playing on Friday, I must have a new gown"— but I don't listen, not anymore—the morphine makes me remember: when they brought me the stewed prunes this morning, it all came back to me, those puckery French prunes when I was a boy and how they made my mouth water, and then I—I—what else?

GERASIM: I'm listening, Ivan Ilych.

IVAN ILYCH: The button, this leather button—see? Feel it—morocco— "Morocco is costly" Father said, "Delicate—don't touch it!" And there was a quarrel about it. No, that was some other morocco. Another time, when I tore Fathers' portfolio and was punished…and Mama brought me some tarts….

(GERASIM *rubs.*)

GERASIM: Sleep now, Ivan Ilych.

IVAN ILYCH: …What? No, I'm afraid. Stay here. Stay!

GERASIM: I'm here. I'm here. Where should I go?

IVAN ILYCH: All lies. It's all lies…ahh. What else? What else did he teach you, hmm, your grandpa?

(GERASIM *massages, and recalls, slipping into his old grandfather's voice.*)

GERASIM: Ahhh…"Without Jesus Christ, the people cannot live and will not die."

IVAN ILYCH: He said that? More. Tell me everything. I don't want to drop off. I'm afraid to sleep—I'm afraid of the Black Bag, the black hole, pushing me down— keep me awake, son, for the love of God!

(GERASIM *is stricken,* IVAN ILYCH *could be dying at this moment!*)

GERASIM: Your Honor, look, look at me—this is how he prayed at night, sometimes wearing a chain, look—

IVAN ILYCH: What? A chain?

(GERASIM *strips off his shirt and mimes whipping himself with a rope.*)

GERASIM: He did, and sometimes he whipped himself with a rope—like this—see, master, and cried out, "Oh God, forgive my enemies!" Then he bowed down in the old way and knocked his head on the floor, like this, "Forgive me, O Lord, teach me how to live, teach me how to live!"

IVAN ILYCH: *(Echoing)* …how to live…how to live…

(GERASIM *bathes* IVAN ILYCH's *face.*)

GERASIM: Then he would tickle me and say that he was "God's fool" and we would laugh.

IVAN ILYCH: *(Laughing)* "God's fool."

GERASIM: And that we must "become fools for Jesus Christ." And then he would kiss me and blow out the candle, and I would go to sleep.

(IVAN ILYCH *is almost unconscious.*)

IVAN ILYCH: …God's fool…

(GERASIM *kisses* IVAN ILYCH *and makes the sign of the cross.*)

(IVAN ILYCH *falls into a restless slumber.* GERASIM *sings an old prison song in a soft bass, thus revealing that his grandfather may at one time have been incarcerated.*)

(IVAN ILYCH's *son,* VASYA, *creeps up the steps and into the room, takes his father's hand to kiss.* GERASIM *strokes both father and son as he sings.*)

GERASIM: "The sun rises and sets
But in my prison cell no light.

"The watchers are watching
Watching closely day and night…"

IVAN ILYCH: …prison? That's a prison song…

(The dying man's eyes open wide. GERASIM crosses himself as he sings. IVAN ILYCH sinks back, groaning.)

Scene Fifteen Dream, 4 A M that night

(The song becomes an organ sounding. On the screens: symbols and colors and shapes for "IT" and the Black Bag.)

(IVAN ILYCH's groans are near screams now. He is screaming the word "Lies," until only the cutting vowel sound "ie" is heard.)

(These death cries are, at the same time, the birth pangs of IVAN ILYCH and his new life.)

(In the nightmare, GERASIM and VASYA mime whipping IVAN ILYCH with ropes. IVAN ILYCH screams and stumbles from screen to screen: from Black Bag to kidney to appendix to IT.)

(Note: IVAN ILYCH's screams are those sharp, involuntary cries that were heard in the dark before the action began, at the beginning of this story. Church bells begin.)

(Screams, bells, whipping, the organ music—climax and blackout. In the dark, church bells, alone.)

Scene Sixteen
The next morning

(GERASIM hurries in with a shaving bowl and razor. IVAN ILYCH stares at him. When he speaks, his voice is near to a croak.)

IVAN ILYCH: What's that?

GERASIM: A good clean shave, master, that'll make you—

IVAN ILYCH: The stink. —So, it's too much even for you. *(To himself)* I'm a corpse, a living corpse.

(GERASIM *ignores the doomed, deeply depressed tones; he proceeds to spread a towel over his helpless master, and begins to scrape clean the areas around* IVAN ILYCH's *beard.*)

(Off, the sound of young VASYA *trying to play the cello.)*

GERASIM: You'll feel more yourself—let me, now.

IVAN ILYCH: Myself! That's just it. Who am I? A living corpse! ...The good boy who became the good student, the good man, the "good" husband, the great judge: *Ecce Homo!* You'd better cut my throat! Ha-ha!

GERASIM: Give over, master. Turn this way, now, that's it. Almost finished.

(IVAN ILYCH *pulls off the towel and tries to sit up, his voice rising—*)

IVAN ILYCH: Myself! Me! Me came first—and second—and *third*! "Society"! —We were living corpses and we never knew it. Shaved and bathed every morning, smelling of English leather and rose water, clean hands—that's enough now—and I sat in judgment on men in the docks—no more! —And I no more saw them or knew them as human beings than these doctors know me—or my family or colleagues, no, all they knew was the English soap and the sweet smell of the "costume" they called "Your Honor Ivan Ilych Golovin"—Husband, Father, Christian...

(IVAN ILYCH *holds onto* GERASIM, *who hums and rocks him. Finally, in a small voice,* IVAN ILYCH *begins again.*)

IVAN ILYCH: ...Your grandpa...

GERASIM: Rest, now—

IVAN ILYCH: He died—

GERASIM: *(Cleaning up the room)* Aye, he—

IVAN ILYCH: When he died, did he suffer, did he—

GERASIM: Shh—he never said. He died quiet, like a man, no fuss.... He gave me his tools.

IVAN ILYCH: *(Pause)* He made a good end.

GERASIM: Aye, aye.

(Now, GERASIM begins to clip his master's fingernails. IVAN ILYCH watches the lad closely.)

IVAN ILYCH: He, ah, how do the old believers say it? He left "a clean smell after him".

GERASIM: Aye, that's it. He did. That's just what he did. He blessed each one of us— "I'll find my freedom in God" —That's all he said...

(GERASIM finishes clipping. The two men stare at each other. Silence. IVAN ILYCH's breathing is shallow; he is struggling to say something.)

IVAN ILYCH: ...Ah, hah—here it is: Your grandpa, and you, too—my people, we called you sweaty and smelling and dirty, called you "the dark ones" —but you were, in truth, clean! And your grandfather left a clean odor after him—and me, me! —me and my people, what have we left? He gave you his tools! — The storm is coming—we all know that—and what tools have I to leave! What can I leave my son? What? A catechism of worn out elite rubbish, etiquette and copy book maxims—in French! —how to make himself, *just comme il faut*, to dance the dance of privilege and power—to play at being judges and gods when we were not even men—so that, in the end, my poor boy can die like me, like a dog, and then they will bury him in *his* medals, his ribbons—

(They stare at each other. Silence. Then, GERASIM *drops to his knees at* IVAN ILYCH's *feet.)*

IVAN ILYCH: No! Get up! What are you doing?!

GERASIM: Your feet.

IVAN ILYCH: *What?!*

GERASIM: Time to clip your toenails, Ivan Ilych—

*(*IVAN ILYCH *gives out a strangled cry of hysterical laughter. The laugh is transformed into a scream as the lights blackout.)*

Scene Seventeen
Winter, 1883. 1 P M. Death

*(*IVAN ILYCH *lies in a cold, winter window light. His screams—after three days!—are, now, only a rasping echo of his nightmare.)*

*(*GERASIM *hurries in to try to prepare his master for the* DOCTOR *and family: the last visit. Now, he puts a rag in the Judge's mouth and the screams sink to a low threnody. As* GERASIM *tries to compose* IVAN ILYCH, *the* DOCTOR, PRASKOVYA FEDOROVNA, LISA, *her fiancée,* VASYA, *and a* PRIEST, *make their entrance. They stand on the steps but do not enter onto the platform. Church bells)*

(The DOCTOR *enters, at last, and with* GERASIM's *aid gives opium to the patient. As the* DOCTOR *retreats to the steps, he confides to the family:)*

DOCTOR: ...A large dose.

PRASKOVYA FEDOROVNA: My dear...Vanya...will you do something for me?

(Starting to groan again, her husband looks at her.)

IVAN ILYCH: Forgive me...

PRASKOVYA FEDOROVNA: It can't do any harm. The priest is here.

(IVAN ILYCH *groans.*)

PRASKOVYA FEDOROVNA: Please let him come in.

(IVAN ILYCH *begins to toss and mutter.* PRASKOVYA FEDOROVNA *takes this as a sign of assent and waves the* PRIEST *in, then she gestures all the rest to leave.*)

(*Alone, the* PRIEST *enters, makes the sign of the cross and begins the last rites.*)

PRIEST: "...Lord have mercy on him
Christ have mercy on him..."

(*The* YOUNG IVAN ILYCH, *[Vasya], and his mother, [*PRASKOVYA FEDOROVNA*], appear in another stage area. The boy, in pajamas, is saying his prayers to his mother.*)

YOUNG IVAN ILYCH: ...God bless Mamma and Papa, and Nikolai and Natasha...

(*Simultaneously, the* PRIEST *continues with the last rites, on the platform.*)

PRIEST: "...John the Baptist pray for him
All you holy Virgins and Women pray for him..."

(*Simultaneously:*)

YOUNG IVAN ILYCH: ...and God bless Sailor and Gypsy...

(*Simultaneously, on the platform:*)

PRIEST: "...and all you Saints and Hermits
All you holy Widows and Orphans..."

(*Simultaneously:*)

YOUNG IVAN ILYCH: ...forgive us our sins, and help me to be a good boy...

(*Fade out on mother and son in an embrace. On the platform:*)

PRIEST: "...Lord have mercy on us
Christ have mercy—"

(*Suddenly,* IVAN ILYCH *screams out.*)

IVAN ILYCH: No!

(*The* PRIEST *rushes the rite and runs out. The "O" vowel in "no" is now the sound of* IVAN ILYCH's *screams.*)

(GERASIM *hurries in and rocks* IVAN ILYCH *in his arms.*)

(*From within the house can be heard the crying and sobbing of the family.*)

IVAN ILYCH: —No! —No! —O! —O! —O!

(GERASIM *rocks, and sings louder than the hoarse screams.*)

GERASIM: "The sun rises and sets
But in my prison cell no light..."

(*At last,* IVAN ILYCH's *voice gives out. He gasps for breath. With his last strength, he lifts his lips to* GERASIM's *ear.*)

IVAN ILYCH: Mamma...forgive me...

GERASIM: "In the name of the Father and of the Son and of the Holy Spirit."

(IVAN ILYCH *rubs a leather button on the couch.*)

IVAN ILYCH: Mamma...Morocco's expensive—Papa's angry—I tore his portfolio—forgive me...

GERASIM: "And he that was dead came forth..."

IVAN ILYCH: ...Help my son—tell him—tell him that Caius was a man...

GERASIM: "Loose him and let him go..."

IVAN ILYCH: ...Mamma—did you bring me a tart—is Papa still angry? (*He begins to shake.*)

GERASIM: "Then said the Jews, Behold how he loved him!"

IVAN ILYCH: Mamma, I'm afraid of the Black Sack—
(He is in absolute terror.)

GERASIM: "Jesus wept."

(GERASIM *embraces him, to control* IVAN ILYCH's *convulsions.*)

IVAN ILYCH: —I love you and Papa— Put me in— Put me into the Black Bag—Mamma— *Put me in!*

(GERASIM *embraces* IVAN ILYCH. *The death throes are like a birth ordeal.* GERASIM *and* IVAN ILYCH *thrash together on the couch.*)

IVAN ILYCH: *Put me in!*

GERASIM: "Come out of the man!"

IVAN ILYCH: Ahhh!—I'm in—I'm in—*Mamma, I'm in!*— kiss me on the mouth!

(GERASIM *kisses* IVAN ILYCH *on the mouth.*)

(*Time stops for* IVAN ILYCH. *He looks into the youth's face and he sees: all the truth of* GERASIM's *love; then, his mother's visage; then, Christ's; and, finally,* GERASIM, *again.*)

(*Each revelation shakes* IVAN ILYCH *to his core. Excrutiatingly, over a span of five seconds,* IVAN ILYCH *arches—stiffens—stretches out—dies.*)

(GERASIM *holds* IVAN ILYCH *in a long, frozen embrace. Then, he lowers the corpse down to the couch. Now, he bows his head to the floor, like the Old Believers, and prays:*)

GERASIM: "To the Father, and the Son, and the Holy Spirit…"

(GERASIM *rises and touches the leather button on the couch, then closes* IVAN ILYCH's *eyes. Finally, he sings a verse of the prison song to numb his pain and loss.*)

GERASIM: "…The watchers are watching
Watching closely day and night…"

(Silence. GERASIM *gathers his strength: rises, picks up the full commode, descends the steps carefully—and reenters the world and the storm that he knows is coming....)*

(The cello, off, and a long fade to darkness)

END OF PLAY

www.ingramcontent.com/pod-product-compliance
Lightning Source LLC
Chambersburg PA
CBHW072017060426
42446CB00043B/2658